T0345570

Poems

THE GERMAN LIST

GEORG TRAKL

Poems

Book One of Our Trakl

TRANSLATED BY JAMES REIDEL

LONDON NEW YORK CALCUTTA

 **GOETHE-INSTITUT**

This publication was supported by a grant from
the Goethe-Institut India

Grateful acknowledgement is made to the following
publications in which these translations first appeared:

Mudlark: 'Concertino', 'In an Old Guest Book', 'Mankind',
'Melancholy', 'Metamorphosis'

Trinity Journal of Literary Translation: 'De profundis', 'Psalm'.

Seagull Books, 2015

Translation © James Reidel, 2015

ISBN 978 0 8574 2 246 0

British Cataloguing-in-Publication Data

A catalogue record for this book is available
from the British Library

Typeset in Adobe Caslon Pro by Seagull Books, Calcutta, India
Printed and bound at Maple Press, York, Pennsylvania, USA

Contents

Translator's Note

To mark the 2014 centenary of the death of the poet Georg Trakl (1887–1914), I have rendered the Austrian Expressionist's first book, titled simply *Poems* (*Gedichte*), published by Kurt Wolff in 1913. Unlike previous translations, I wanted to present Trakl's debut as close as possible to the original experience, even its historicity, while seeing him as a poet bridging two centuries and yet having an ear for the future—where we find ourselves. His declinism, set during the final years of Imperial Austria, is just as relevant today.

Also, I want my renderings to have the same concentrated *manie*, in keeping with the poets Trakl read from the previous century—Baudelaire, Rimbaud, Verlaine, Hölderlin, Poe. This quality is often thinly presented or lost in selected and collected editions. I want to actually channel Trakl, his craft (with its implicit painterliness) and work ethic, to have him, so to speak, absorbed in the right dosages he—as a poet, pharmacist and addict—intended.

In my research, I pored over the correspondence between Trakl and Wolff at Yale's Beinecke Library, I could see that Trakl wanted his work consumed in a certain order, line by line. Thus I have tried to emulate his delivery with a certain prosody and diction in English that bears as much resemblance to the original as possible. While this comes with the sacrifice of Trakl's original rhyme scheme in many poems, the triteness that often comes of such a valiant attempt to impose one is avoided.

Poems is the first book in a cycle, which is titled 'Our Trakl' for the many attempts to render, read and appropriate his work into English, while what this poet means is liminal, often personal, and his alone. That said, his influence on our poetry is immeasurable.

Poems (1913)

The Ravens

With harsh caws above the black valley,
The ravens make haste during the midday.
Their shadow passing over stripes a doe
And sometimes you see them roosting restive.

O how they disturb the brown stillness,
Where plowed acres know bliss like a woman
Rapt by a cruel premonition,
And sometimes they can be heard to bicker

Over a carcass they sense somewhere,
And suddenly point to the north in flight
And recede like a funeral cortege
Into winds tingling with ecstasy.

The Young Maid
Dedicated to Ludwig von Ficker

1

Often at the well when it gets light,
You see her standing in a trance
Dipping water when it gets light.
The buckets go up and go down.

In the beeches jackdaws flutter
And they resemble a shadow.
Her yellow hair is aflutter
And the rats squeal inside the farm.

And she flattered by the ruin
Lowers her enkindled eyelids.
The withered grass in the ruin
Bends over to bow at her feet.

2

She works silent inside her cell
And the farm lies long deserted.
In the elder tree from her cell
Plaintively a blackbird whistles.

Her silver image in the mirror
Gives her a strange look in twilight
And fades pallid in the mirror
And its purity frightens her.

Dreamlike a farmhand in the dark
Sings and she stares shaken with pain.
Red bleeds away into the dark.
Then the south wind rattles the gate.

3

At night on the barren meadow
She flits across in fevered dreams.
The restive winds whine in the meadow
And the moon listens from the trees.

Soon the encircling stars will fade
And wearying of the hardship
Her waxen cheeks begin to fade.
From the earth rot senses something.

Reeds rustle sadly in the pond
And she freezes cringing inside.
Far off a cock crows. Over the pond
The morning shivers harsh and grey.

4

Inside the forge clangs the hammer
And she darts past the entranceway.
Red hot the farmhand swings the hammer
And like death she looks from outside.

Like a dream she's met with laughter;
She wavers entering the forge,
Shrinking scared of his laughter
Like the hammer hard and crude.

Inside the room the fiery sparks
Fly and with a helpless gesture
She reaches after the wild sparks
And falls lifelessly to the ground.

5

Stretched out slender upon the bed
She wakes full of sweet disquiet
And she regards her squalid bed
Draped entirely in golden light,

Mignonettes there in the window
And the blue brightness of the sky.
Sometimes the wind at the window
Brings a bell's shy tintinnabulation.

Shadows glide over the pillow,
Slowly peals the midday hour
And she breathes hard into the pillow
And her mouth resembles a wound.

6

By evening hang the bloody sheets,
Clouds drift over the mute forests,
Which are shrouded over in black sheets.
Sparrows clamour out in the fields.

And she lays all white in the dark.
Under the roof a coo breathes out.
Like a carcass in the brush and dark
Flies swarm milling around her mouth.

Like a dream in the brown hamlet
Hangs a ring of dance and violins,
As her face floats through the hamlet,
As her hair blows in bare branches.

Romance by Night

Under the canopy of stars
One lone walks in the still midnight.
The boy wakes from his dreams confused,
His face sloughs off grey in the moon.

The mad girl weeps with loosened hair
At the window bristling with bars.
On the pond drifts a sweet outing,
The wonder of lovers going by.

The murderer's wine smiles back white,
A horror of death grips the sick.
The nun prays wounded and naked
Before the Saviour's cross of pain.

The mother in her sleep sings low.
The child looks calmly at the night
With eyes that are the utter truth.
Laughter's heard inside the brothel.

In the cellar window's daylight
The dead man paints with a white hand
A leering silence on the wall.
The sleeper goes on whispering.

Among the Red Leaves Full of Guitars . . .

Among the red leaves full of guitars
The yellow hair of the girls flutters
On the fence where the sunflowers stand.
A golden tumbril wheels through the clouds.

In the calm of brown shadows fall silent
The elders, stupidly arm in arm.
The orphans sweetly sing at vespers.
Flies buzz about in clouds of yellow.

At the brook women still do the wash.
The sheets hung up billow in and out.
The little girl long my favourite one
Comes again through that grey of evening.

Sparrows diving from out of fair skies
Plunge into green holes full of decay.
The starved is deceived of being made whole
By a smell of bread and pungent spice.

Music in the Mirabell

A fountain sings. The clouds stack up
Into the clear blue, ones white, wispy.
People slowly promenade hushed
Through the old garden in the evening.

The marbles of ancestors grey.
Passing birds stretch into the distance.
A faun with dead eyes contemplates
Shadows slipping into the darkness.

The leaves fall red from an old tree
And spiral through an open window.
Firelight flares in a room and paints
Chaotic fearsome apparitions.

A white stranger enters the house.
A dog bounds through ruined passageways.
The maid extinguishes a lamp,
The ear follows sonata notes all night.

Melancholy of the Evening

—The forest that spreads already dead—
And shadows surround it like hedgerows.
Trembling wild deer come from hiding
While a stream drifts in utter silence

And follows the ferns and the old stones
And gleams silver from garlands of leaves.
Soon you hear it in the black gorges—
Perhaps so that the stars appear too.

The dark plain appears without measure,
Scattered villages, marshland and pond,
And something fools you facing a fire.
A cold splendour darts over the streets.

You anticipate the sky to stir,
A host of wild birds in migration
To these lands, beautiful, different.
The stirring of the reeds rises and falls.

Winter Twilight
To Max von Esterle

The black heavens of metal.
In the evening hunger-mad crows
Are drifting crosswise in red storms
Over parks sad and ashen.

Sunlight dies of cold in the clouds;
And those before Satan's curses
Spin in a circle and descend
In a number sevenfold.

In rot that is sweet and stale
Their beaks shear without any sound.
Houses loom in mute imminence;
Brightness in the theatre hall.

Churches, bridges, a hospital
Tower grisly in the twilight.
Sheets spattered with blood are filling
The sails out on the canal.

Rondel

The gold of these days melted away,
The brown and blue colours of evening:
The gentle pipes of the shepherd died
The brown and blue colours of evening
The gold of these days melted away.

Boon of Women

You walk among your women
And often smile hesitantly:
Days of such worry are ahead.
Poppies bloom white by the fence.

Like your belly swelled so fair,
So the grapes on the hill ripen.
The pond's surface shines from afar
And the scythe snicks in the field.

The dew beads in the greenery,
The leaves are streaming down red.
Greeting his dear wife a black man
Approaches you brown and raw.

The Beautiful City

Old sunny squares keep the silence.
Spun deep into the blue and gold
Meek nuns hasten like in a dream
In the beeches' stifling silence.

From the lights inside brown churches
Peer the pure images of death,
Beautiful shields of great princes.
Crowns shimmer within the churches.

Horses surface from the fountain.
Petalled claws menace from the trees.
Boys play quietly in a daze
From their dreams there by the fountain.

Girls standing around by the gates
Look shyly at life in colour.
Their moistened lips are aquiver
As they wait around by the gates.

Bell peals flutter tremulously,
A march beat sounds and sentries call.

The tourists listen on the steps.
Organ notes are high in the blue.

Gleaming instruments are singing.
From through the garden's frame of leaves
Purrs the laughter of fine ladies.
Soft-voiced young mothers are singing.

A furtive scent by flowered windows
Whispers incense, tar and lilacs.
Weary eyelids flutter silver
Through flowers along the windows.

In a Deserted Room

A window, vibrant flower beds,
From inside an organ plays.
Shadows dance on the wallpaper
Into a bizarrely mad ring dance.

The hedgerows blow into a blaze,
And a swarm of gnats takes wing.
Scythes mow out in the distant field,
And an age-old water sings.

Whose breathing comes to flirt with me?
Swallows trace their manic signs.
Softly into infinity
There flows this golden woodland.

Flames are flickering in the beds.
The mad ring rapt in a whir
On the yellowish wallpaper.
Someone watches in the door.

The incense smells sweet and the pears
And mirror and chest grow dim.
Slowly the burning brow submits
Itself to the white stars too.

To the Boy Elis

Elis, when the blackbird calls in the black forest,
This is your going down.
Your lips sip the cold of the blue spring in the rocks.

Let it be when your brow quietly bleeds
Archaic legends
And the dark augur of birds in the sky.

But you walk with such yielding steps into the night,
Which sags full of purple grapes
And you sway your arms handsome in the blue.

A thorn bush is heard
Where your moon eyes are.
O, how long, Elis, you are dead.

Your body is a hyacinth,
In which a monk dips waxen fingers.
A black den is our silence,

From which a gentle beast appears at times
And slowly the heavy lids droop.
Upon your temples drips black dew,

The dying gold of ruined stars.

The Stormy Evening

O the red hours of the evening!
Grape leaves in an open window
Flicker wild twisting in the blue,
Within them nest fearsome spectres.

Dust dances in the gutters' reek.
Wind pushes at the rattling panes.
Thunderbolts drive the dazzling clouds
Into a stampede of wild horses.

The pond's reflection shatters loud.
Seagulls cry in the window frames.
A fiery rider bolts downhill
And explodes amid the fir trees.

Patients scream in the hospital.
The plumage of night rustles blue.
All at once the rain showers down
Glittering over the rooftops.

Evening Muse

Amid the window's flowers the church steeple's shadow
And goldenness return. The hot brow burns in peace and
    silence.
A fountain cascades in the darkness of the chestnut limbs;
Here, in your painful lethargy, you feel it is good!

The market is emptied out of summer fruit and wreaths.
The black retinue of the gates is in unison.
In a garden the sounds of a gentle game are heard,
Where friends find themselves together after suppertime.

The soul loves listening to the white magician's tale.
Grain sings all around that reapers cut this afternoon.
The hard life in the cottages forebears in silence;
The stall lantern shines upon the cattle's gentle sleep.

Made drunk by the skies, the eyelids subside before long
And open softly on the strange signs among the stars.
Endymion rises from the gloom of ancient oaks
And lowers himself over funereal waters.

Dream of Evil

Falling unheard the brown-gold strikes of a gong—
In rooms that are black a lover is waking,
Cheek to the flames that flicker in the window.
Out there on the river dazzle sails, masts, rigging.

There in the crowd a monk, a pregnant woman.
Guitars are strumming, red skirts are shimmering.
Sweltering chestnuts wilt in golden splendour;
The funereal pomp of churches rears black.

From pale masks the ghost of evil is watching.
A plaza grows dark dreadful and sepulchral;
On the islands a whisper stirs in the evening.

Reading the scattered signs in flocks of birds
Are lepers perhaps festering in the night.
In the park, siblings glimpse each other trembling.

Hymn

Signs, a blustery flowerbed
Paints strange embroidery.
The blue breath of God blows
Inside the garden ballroom,
Bright inside.
A cross juts from the wild grapes.

In the village hear their joy,
A gardener mows by the wall,
An organ quietly goes,
Commingling sound and gold light,
Sound and light.
Love blesses the bread and wine.

Young girls also come inside
And the cock crows to the last.
A rotten trellis gently goes,
And in rose crown and garlands,
Rose garlands,
Lies Mary white and frail.

Beggars against an old stone
Seem dead in prayer, a herdsman

Goes meekly from the hillside
And an angel in the grove,
The near grove,
Sings the children there to sleep.

In Autumn

The sunflowers blaze along the fence,
The patients sit still in the sunshine.
Women labour singing in the field,
To which the bells of the cloister toll.

The birds tell you of faraway myths,
To which the bells of the cloister toll.
From the yard a violin softly tunes.
Today they are pressing the brown wine.

Here one turns out bright and light.
Today they are pressing the brown wine.
The dead houses have been opened wide
And painted beautiful with sunshine.

My Heart towards Evening

At dusk one hears the squeak of the bats.
Two black horses leap in the meadow.
The red maple rustles.
To the wanderer appears a small tavern on the way.
Splendid how new wine and nuts taste.
Splendid: to be reeling drunk in the gloaming forest.
Through the black branches ring the painful bells.
Dew beads on the face.

The Peasants

Green and red echo outside the window.
In the black smoke-filled hall in the rear
Farmhands and maids sit around their meal;
And they pour wine and they break the bread.

In the deep silence of the noon hour,
Every now and then a spare word falls.
The fields scintillate on and on
And the sky that is leaden and wide.

Coals flicker fearsomely in the hearth
And a swarm of flies bustle.
The farm girls listen foolish and hushed
And the blood hammers at their temples.

And sometimes their eyes meet full of greed,
When a brutal haze drifts through the room.
A farmhand prays in a monotone
And a cock crows from under the door.

Again the field. Often a dread grips
Them in the stormy sea of wheat ears

And the scythes keep swinging to and fro
Snicking wraithlike together in time.

All Souls
To Karl Hauer

Little husbands, wives, sombre companions,
On this day they scatter flowers blue and red
On their tombs that have been timidly lit.
They perform like wretched puppets before death.

O! how they look here, full of fear, effacement,
Like shadows standing behind the black hedges.
The unborn's weeping moans in the autumn wind,
You see too the candles walking astray.

The lovers sighing whispers in the branches
And there decays the mother with child.
The ring dance of the ones living seems unreal
And disperses into the evening wind.

Their lives reel so much, filled with dull troubles.
God pity the pain and hell of women,
And this lamenting hopelessly about death.
The alone walk silent in the hall of stars.

Melancholy

Bluishly casting shadows. O you dark eyes,
Who take a long look at me floating on by.
Guitar music softly accompanies autumn
In the garden dissolved in brown soap water.
Nymphish hands stir the utter desolation
Of the dead, lips that are rotting apart
Suckle on red breasts and in black soap water
The locks of the slender youth float in the sun.

Soul of Life

Decay, which softly beclouds the leaves,
Whose vast silence dwells in the woods.
Soon a village appears to bow ghostlike,
The sister's mouth whispers in the black branches.

The lonely man will soon slip away,
Perhaps a herdsman on the dark paths.
A beast steps softly from the trees' colonnade,
While eyelids open wide before the godhead.

The blue stream runs beautifully down,
The clouds come out with the evening;
So also the soul in angelic silence.
Ephemeral creations perish.

Glorious Autumn

The year comes to an end potent
With golden wine and fruit from gardens.
The woods around keep wondrously still
And are the alone's companions.

Now the farmer pronounces: It is good.
You evening bells prolonged and low
Still give blithe courage to the end.
A line of birds hails in passage.

It is that mellow season of love.
In the rowboat down the blue river
How well image builds on image—
Sinking away in peace and silence.

Valley in the Forest
To Karl Minnich

Brown chestnut trees. Quietly the old people float by
On a quieter evening; lovely leaves wither softly.
In the churchyard, the blackbird banters with its dead cousin,
The blonde teacher provides Angela with a chaperone.

Death's immaculate figures watch from stained-glass windows;
Yet a bloody motive seems quite doleful and dreary.
The door remains locked today. The sexton has the key.
In the garden the sister converses warmly with ghosts.

In the old cellar, the wine ages to gold, clarity.
Apples smell sweet. Joy glitters from not so far away.
Children like hearing fairy tales long into the evening;
The gold, truth too often points to mild insanity.

The blue pours mignonettes; candlelight in rooms.
For those who are meek their place is well prepared.
A lonely fate floats down at the edge of the forest;
The night appears, the angel of peace, on the threshold.

In the Winter

The field is alight with white and cold.
The sky is desolate and monstrous.
Jackdaws circle above the pond
And hunters descend from the forest.

A silence dwells in the black treetops.
Firelight darts from the cottages.
Now and then a sleigh jingles way off
And a grey moon slowly rises.

A deer softly bleeds out between fields
And ravens splash in bloody furrows.
The reeds shiver yellow and spindly.
Frost, smoke, a step in the barren grove.

In an Old Guest Book

Time and again you return, melancholy,
O that meekness of the lonely soul.
A golden day blazes to the end.

Fully humbled the uncomplaining bows to pain
Sounding sweet and semi-insane.
See! It's getting dark already.

The night returns and something mortal laments
And something else suffers along.

Shuddering under the autumnal stars
The head lowers deeper with each year.

Metamorphosis

Along a garden, autumnal, red-scorched:
Here in the stillness is shown a proper life.
The people's hands are bearing the brown grapevines,
While the mellow pain in the eyes recedes.

With evening: footfalls go through the black land,
One emerging in the silence of red beech.
A blue creature wishes to bow before death
And an empty robe loathsomely decays.

Something serene plays outside a tavern,
A face has sunken besotted in the grass.
Elderberry fruit, flutes mellow and drunken,
A mignonette scent bathes something female.

Concertino

A red, that's shaking you in a dream—
Through your hands the sun appears to shine.
You feel your heart mad with ecstasy,
Silently ready to do something.

The yellow fields deluge into noon.
You can hardly hear the crickets sing,
The grim wielding of the reapers' scythes.
Golden forests naively keep still.

Decay smoulders in the green temples
The fish keep to a dead calm. God's breath
Gently wakes a string piece in the reek.
Its flood promises health to lepers.

Daedalus' ghost hovers in blue shadows,
A haze of milk in hazel branches.
Still one long hears the teacher strike up,
In the empty yard the cry of rats.

On ghastly public house wallpaper
Blossom cooler shades of violet.

In their discord the dark voices died,
Narcissus in the end chord of flutes.

Mankind

Mankind lined up before fiery maws,
A drumroll, the brows of gloomy warriors,
Footsteps through a blood fog; black iron jingles,
Desperation, night in funereal brains:
Here Eve's shadow, a manhunt and red coin.
Clouds, the light is breaking through, the Last Supper.
A gentle silence dwells in bread and wine.
And those gathered here are twelve in number.
Nights they moan asleep beneath olive boughs;
Saint Thomas dips his hand into the wound.

The Walk

1

Music hums in the grove midafternoon.
Solemn scarecrows twist around in the grain.
Elderberry gently toss on the way;
A house gutters away strange and remote.

A smell of thyme hovers in goldenness,
A buoyant number stands up on a stone.
In a meadow children are playing ball,
Then a tree rises wheeling before you.

You dream: the sister combs her blonde hair out,
A distant friend writes you a letter too.
A haystack flees through grey yellowed and slumped
And sometimes you hover light and wondrous.

2

Time trickles away. O sweet Helios!
O image sweet and clear in the toad pond;
An Eden gloriously sinks in the sand.
A bush cradles gold-hammers in its belly.

A brother to you dies in a cursed land
And your eyes watch you with a steely gaze.
A smell of thyme hangs in the goldenness.
At the hamlet a boy ignites a fire.

The lovers glow anew amid butterflies
And spin gaily around stone and number.
Crows flutter up around a loathsome meal
And your brow explodes through the gentle green.

A deer quietly dies in a thorn bush.
A sunny childhood day floats in your wake,
The grey wind, one fluttering and remote
Washing the rotting smells through the twilight.

3

An old cradlesong gives you such worry.
Wayside a woman bows nursing her child.
Sleepwalking you hear her fountain spurting.
A votive sound falls from apple branches

And the bread and wine are sweet with hard toil.
Your silver hand fumbles among the fruits.
The dead Rachel walks across the ploughland.
The green beckons to the peaceful soil.

Blessed too poor farm girls' bellies in flower,
Who stand there dreaming around the old well.
The solitary walk on the still paths
Overjoyed with God's creatures, without sin.

De Profundis

There is a stubble field in which a black rain falls.
There is a brown tree that stands alone.
There is a whispering wind that circles empty cottages.
How sad this evening.

Past the hamlet
The meek orphan still gleans scant spikes of grain.
Her eyes feast round and precious in the twilight
And her loins await the heavenly bridegroom.

On coming home
The herdsmen found the sweet body
Rotted in the thorn bush.

I am a shadow far from dark villages.
God's silence
I drank from the well of the grove.

Cold metal comes to my brow
Spiders seek my heart.
There is a light put out in my mouth.

Nights I find myself on a heath,
Matted with filth and the dust of stars.
In the hazel bush
Crystalline angels rang once more.

Trumpets

Under clipped willow trees, where brown children play
And drive the leaves, trumpets sound. A churchyard awe.
Banners of scarlet drop through the maples' mourning,
Riders along the rye fields, the abandoned mills.

Or the herdsmen sing during the night and stags step forth
Into the circle of their fire, this grove's ancient sorrow,
The dancers lift themselves from one of the black walls;
Banners of scarlet, laughter, madness, trumpets.

Twilight

In the yard possessed by a milky gloaming,
The tender sick drift through autumn's embrownment.
Their round waxen eyes contemplate golden times,
Filled with daydreaming, tranquillity and wine.

Their incurableness entraps them wraithlike.
The stars disperse a white melancholia.
In the grey, astir with delusion and bells,
Watch how the afflicted scatter in turmoil.

Formless figures of ridicule dart, cower
And they flutter up along the black crossed paths.
O! what miserable shadows on the wall.

Others flee through the darkening colonnades;
And at night they come rushing from red showers
Of the stellar wind like furious maenads.

Bright Spring

1

By the brook through the yellow fallow field,
The thin reeds from the year past still rise up.
Through the grey the sounds drift full of wonder,
A whisper of warm manure breezes past.

Pussy willows dangle softly in the wind,
A soldier dreamily sings his sad song.
A strip of grassland hisses tossed and faint,
A child stands limned in lines supple and soft.

The birches there and the black thorn bushes,
Shapes are fleeing dissolved in smoke as well.
One bright green flourishes, another rots
And toads are sleeping throughout the young leeks.

2

I love you true, you hard washerwoman,
The flood still carries the sky's golden burden.
A small fish flashes past and fades away;
A waxen face escapes through the alder.

In the gardens bells subside long and low.
A little bird trills as if it were mad.
The mellow grain increases soft and rapt
And bees still gather fiercely thorough.

Come now love to the weary labourer!
A warm shaft of light falls inside his hut.
The forest flows through evening harsh and pale
And the buds split open brightly now and then.

3

How all the expectancy seems so sick!
A feverish breath surrounds the hamlet;
But a meek ghost beckons in the branches
And opens the being within wide and scared.

A florid effusion drips very softly out
And the unborn tends to his proper sleep.
The lovers are flowering into their stars
And their sweet breath escapes through the night.

What lives is so painfully good and real;
And an ancient stone quietly moves you:
Truly! I will be by your side for ever.
O mouth! aquiver through silver willows.

Outskirts in the Föhn

The place lies dead and brown with evening,
The air permeated with a ghastly stench.
From the viaduct the rumble of a train—
And sparrows flutter across hedge and fence.

Low cottages, paths scattered in a maze,
In the gardens disarray and commotion,
Sometimes a howl rises out of some vague urge,
In a crowd of children a frock flies red.

A rat choir squeaks love-struck in the garbage,
Women carry bushel baskets of offal,
A sickening parade replete with filth and scabs,
They materialize from the twilight.

A canal suddenly spews congealed blood
From the slaughterhouse into the still river.
The föhn gives the few sparse wildflowers more colour
And slowly the redness creeps through the flood.

A whisper, one that drowns in muddled sleep.
Shapes come staggering up out of the ditches,
Perhaps some memory of an earlier life,
One that rises and falls with the warm winds.

Shining avenues come out of the clouds,
Filled with fine chariots, bold charioteers.
One sees too a ship foundered upon the cliffs
And every now and then rose-coloured mosques.

The Rats

The autumn moon shines white in the yard.
Fantastic shadows are falling from the eaves.
A silence dwells in empty windows;
Then the rats softly surface from below

And they dart squeaking here and there
And a ghastly reek from the outhouse
Follows them picking up their scent,
Shivering eerily through the moonlight

And they bicker like mad with greed
And they overrun house and barns,
Those that burst with grain stores and crops.
Icy winds howl in the darkness.

Gloom

A world of trouble haunts the afternoon.
Hovels flee through garden plots brown and bare.
Votive lights flit about the dung fire's coals,
Two sleepers stagger home grey and remote.

A child races across the withered grass
And plays with his eyes that go black and smooth.
The gold drips from bushes dull and tarnished.
An old man's spinning sadly in the wind.

Once more with evening over my head,
Saturn mutely governs a wretched fate.
A tree, a dog backs away behind it
And God's heaven staggers black and leafless.

A little fish darts quickly beneath the stream;
And the dead friend's hand quietly rises
And lovingly smooths his forehead and robe.
A light awakens shadows in the room.

Whispered during the Afternoon

Sun, autumnal, thin and shy,
And the fruit falls from the trees.
Stillness dwells within its blue rooms
During a long afternoon.

Death knells booming of metal;
And a white animal goes down.
The raucous ballads of brown girls
Blow away in falling leaves.

God's brow dreams of these colours,
Feels the delirium's soft wing.
Shadows swirl around on the hill
Of decay bordered in black.

A twilight full of sleep and wine;
Tragic guitars pour themselves out.
And towards the kind light within
You drop by like in a dream.

Psalm
Dedicated to Karl Kraus

There is a candle that the wind has blown out.
There is a tavern-on-the-heath from which a drunk departs in
    the afternoon.
There is a vineyard burnt and black with holes full of spiders.
There is a room that they have whitewashed with milk.
The maniac is dead. There is an island in the South Seas
To welcome the sun god. Someone is beating drums.
The men perform war dances.
The women sway their hips in creeping vines and fire blossoms
When the sea sings. O our lost paradise.

The nymphs have forsaken the golden woods.
Someone buries the stranger. Then a glittering rain commences.
The son of Pan appears disguised as a ditch digger
Sleeping through noon on the burning asphalt.
In the courtyard there are little girls in little dresses rife with
    heart-rending poverty.
There is a room filled with chord runs and sonatas.
There are shadows that embrace themselves before a blind
    mirror.

In the windows of the hospital the patients warm themselves.
A white steamer brings bloody plagues up the canal.

The strange sister reappears in someone's bad dreams.
Sleeping in the hazel bush she toys with his stars.
The student, perhaps a double, gazes after her for a long time
    from the window.
Behind him stands his dead brother, or he goes down the old
    spiral stairs.
In the dark of brown chestnuts the figure of the young novitiate
    wanes.
The garden is in dusk. Bats flutter about the cloister yard.
The caretaker's children stop playing and search for the gold
    of heaven.
A quartet's end-chords. The little blind girl runs unsteadily
    through the alley,
And later her shadow fingers cold walls, surrounded by fairy
    tales and holy legends.

There is an empty boat that drifts down the black canal during
    the evening.
In the gloom of the old asylum human ruins decay.
The dead orphans lie against the garden wall.
From grey rooms angels appear with shit-spattered wings.
Worms drop from their yellowed eyelids.
The plaza outside the church is sinister and silent as in the days
    of childhood.
On their silver feet previous lives glide past

And the shadows of the damned climb down into the sighing
    waters.
In his grave the white magician dandles his snakes.

Silently over Golgotha God's golden eyes open.

Rosary Hymns

'To My Sister'

Where you walk will be autumn and evening,
A blue deer that is heard under the trees,
A lonely pond in the evening.

Softly the flight of birds is heard,
The sadness above the orbits of your eyes.
Your narrow smile is heard.

God crinkled your eyelids.
Stars seek the night, Good Friday's child,
The arches of your brows.

'Nearness of Death'

O that evening that enters the grim villages of childhood.
The pond under the willows
Fills itself with the pestilent sighs of melancholy.

O the forest that softly lowers brown eyes,
While from the hands of the alone
The crimson of his rapturous days falls impotent.

O the nearness of death. Let us pray.
During this night on cool pillows
The lovers' slender limbs free themselves yellowed by incense.

'Amen'

Cadaverousness drifting through the ruined parlour;
Shadows on yellow wallpaper; in dark mirrors
Arches the ivory sadness of our hands.

Brown beads slip through dead fingers.
In the stillness
The blue poppy eyes of an angel open.

Blue is the evening too;
The hour of our death, Azrael's shadow,
Which eclipses a small brown garden.

Decay

In the evening, when the bells toll of peace,
I follow the birds in their glorious flights,
Long multitudes, like pious trains of pilgrims,
Disappearing into autumn's clear breadths.

Wandering through the twilight-filled garden
I dream following their brighter destinies
And feel the sundials barely move any more.
So I follow their journeys above the clouds.

There a blast of decay makes me start to tremble.
The blackbird laments in the leafless branches.
The red vine totters on rusting trellises

While, like a dance of death of pale children
Around the dark weathered rim of the fountain,
The blue asters toss shivering in the wind.

At Home

Mignonette notes stray through the sick window;
An old plaza, chestnuts black and ugly.
A golden shaft penetrates the roof and pours
On siblings in a dream and in a daze.

Decay floats in wash water, the föhn wind
Softly coos in the brown garden; the sunflower
Very still relishes its gold and dissolves.
The sentry's call rattles through the blue air.

Mignonette notes. The walls light up barrenly.
The sister's sleep is heavy. Night wind wallows
In her hair, the moon glow splashes around.

The cat's shadow slips blue and lithe off the roof,
Rotted, holding back coming disaster,
The candle flame which rears itself up red.

An Autumn Evening
To Karl Röck

The brown village. A dark thing often appears
Loping along walls still in the autumn,
Shapes: male as well as female, the dead going
Inside the cool rooms to make ready their bed.

The boys play here. Heavy shadows spread across
A brown pool of manure. The milkmaids walk
Through the damp blue and sometimes they see it
From eyes filling with the tolling of the night.

There is a tavern here for the alone,
Holding back patiently under the dark arches
Surrounded by gold clouds of tobacco.

But one's own self is always black and near.
That drunk in the shadows of the old arches
Contemplates the wild birds, those that flew afar.

Human Misery

The clock that's tolling five before the sun—
A dark horror takes hold of lonely people,
Leafless trees sough in the evening garden.
The corpse's face rouses at the window.

Perhaps so that this hour will stand still.
Before glazed eyes blue images flit about
In the pitch and roll of boats on the river.
A flock of nuns breezes by on the quay.

In the hazel trees girls play pale and blind,
As if they were lovers embracing in sleep.
Perhaps so that flies sing around rotting meat,
That a child cries too in its mother's lap.

The asters fall from the hands blue and red,
The young man's jaw sags open strangely and wise;
And eyelids flutter soft and apprehensive;
A smell of bread drifts through a fever's black.

It seems a dreadful shriek is heard as well;
Skeletons are shimmering through ruined walls.

An evil heart laughs loud in beautiful rooms;
To a dreamer, a dog comes running past.

An empty coffin fades into the dark.
A room casts a pale light on the murderer,
While lanterns shatter during the storm at night.
Laurels grace the ennobled's white temple.

In the Village

1

A village appears from brown walls, a field.
A herdsman rots upon an ancient stone.
The edge of the woods encircles blue beasts,
The gentle leaves that fall in the stillness.

The brown foreheads of the peasants. Long tolls
The evening bells; a pious rite's pretty,
The Redeemer's black head in the brambles,
The cool chamber that propitiates death.

How pale mothers are. The blueness descends
On mirror and chest, proud shrine to its sense;
A white head too, far along in years, bows
On the grandchild who drinks milk and stars.

2

The poor man who died alone in his mind
Surmounts waxen above an ancient path.
The apple trees are sinking stark and still
In the colours of their fruit rotted black.

The roof made of dry thatch ever arches
Above the sleep of cows. The blind milkmaid
Comes out into the yard; blue water wails;
A horse skull stares from a rickety gate.

The idiot darkly utters a word
Of love that goes unheard in a black bush,
Where this person stands in her slim dream form.
The evening's heard in a wetter blue.

3

Föhn-blown leafless limbs beat the windowpanes.
A wild labour swells a farmwife's belly.
Black snow is trickling down into her arms;
Golden-eyed owls flutter about her head.

The walls look on barren and filthy grey
In the cold dark. The pregnant body shivers
In the fever bed, the bold moon watching.
A dog is stretched out dead before her room.

Three men are tramping blackly through the gate
With their scythes broken apart in the field.
Red evening wind rattles through the windows;
Out of this a black angel emerges.

Evening Song

During the evening, when we walk upon dark paths,
Our pale forms appear ahead of us.

When we thirst,
We drink the white waters of the pond,
The sweetness of our sad childhood.

We lie faded away amid the elderberry grove,
Watching the grey gulls.

Spring clouds rise above the gloomy city,
Silencing the monks of nobler times.

As I took your slender hands
You softly open those full eyes,
This happened long ago.

Yet when the soul is haunted by a dark music,
You appear white in this friend's autumnal landscape.

Three Looks into an Opal

To Erhard Buschbeck

1

Look into an opal: a village crowned by withered
    grapevines,
The stillness of grey clouds, of rocky yellow hills,
And wellsprings of evening's coolness: twin mirrors
Framed all around by shadows and slime-covered
    stones.

The autumn's road and crucifixes sink into dusk,
Singing pilgrims and the linen spattered with blood.
Thus the figure of the solitary turns inward
And walks, a pale angel, through the empty orchard.

The föhn wind blows out of the black. Slender women
Are in league with satyrs; monks, the lust's pale priests,
Adorn their madness with lilies both pretty and dark
And lift up their hands to the golden shrine of God.

2

There is hanging saturated in the rosemary
A pink dewdrop: a whisper of reeking graves glides forth,
Of hospitals filled with wild fevered screams and oaths.
Skeletons climb from the family vault frail and grey.

The woman for the old men dances in her blue slime
And veils, the filth-matted hair filled with black tears,
The boys dream entangled in the willow's dry strands
And their foreheads are hairless and raw from leprosy.

Evening falls through the arched window gentle and mild.
A saint steps from the black sores of his stigmata.
The crimson snails crawl out of their cracked open shells
And spit blood in a crown of thorns bristled and grey.

3

The blind scatter incense into festering wounds.
Red-golden vestments; torches; the singing of psalms;
And girls like poison embracing the Lord's body.
Figures stride stiff and waxen through embers and smoke.

In a midnight dance a young fool all skin and bones
Leads the lepers. A garden of wondrous adventures;
Disfigurement; flower faces, laughter; monsters
And an orb revolving inside the black thorn bush.

O poverty, beggars' soup, bread and sweet onions;
Dreaming away one's life in huts facing the woods.
The sky hardens to grey above the yellow fields
And an evening bell carols, keeping with the old ways.

Night Song

The unflinching's breath. A beast's expression
Petrified by the blue, its hallowedness.
Vast is the silence in the stone;

The mask of a night bird. A soft triadic note
Fades into one. Elai! your face
Lowers itself speechless above blue-coloured waters.

O! you still mirrors of the truth.
Upon the ivory temple of one alone
Shines forth the resplendence of fallen angels.

Helian

In the lonely hours of the ghost
There is beauty walking in the sun
Along the yellow walls of the summer.
The footsteps fall quietly in the grass; yet ever sleeps
The son of Pan in the grey marble.

Evenings on the terrace we drank ourselves drunk on brown wine.
The red glow of the peach amid the leaves;
A soft sonata, mirthful laughter.

Beautiful is the stillness of night.
On the dark plain
We meet together with the herdsmen and white stars.

When it becomes autumn
A stark clarity reveals itself in the grove.
We wander calmly along red walls
And our wide eyes follow the flight of birds.
With evening the white water dwindles in the grave urns.

The sky freezes in bare branches.
The peasant brings bread and wine in immaculate hands
And the fruit ripens tranquilly in a sunny room.

O how solemn are the faces of those precious dead.
But it does the soul good by how it does them justice.

Vast is the silence of desolated gardens,
As the young novice crowns the brow with brown leaves,
His breath drinks icy gold.

The hands touch the antiquity of blue waters
Or the white cheeks of the sisters in the cold night.

A corridor is quiet and harmonious between friendly rooms,
Where solitude is and the rustling of the maple tree,
Where, perhaps, the thrush still sings.

In the dark man is beautiful and shining forth,
As he moves arms and legs wide-eyed,
And the eyes roll up calmly in crimson sockets.

At vespers the stranger loses himself in November's black
        devastation,
Under rotten branches, along a wall full of leprosy,
Where before the holy brother had gone,
Drowning in the soft strumming of his madness,

Oh how lonely the autumn wind ends.
The head nods slowly dying in the darkness of the olive trees.

The collapse of our kind is upsetting.
During this hour the eyes of the spectator fill
With the gold of his stars.

A carillon sinks into the evening that no longer tolls,
The black walls on the square are crumbling,
The dead soldier is called to prayer.

A pale angel,
The son enters the empty house of his forefathers.

The sisters have gone to white old men far away.
The sleeper finds them in the night amid the columns in the
    atrium,
Back from sad pilgrimages.

O how stiff their hair is with shit and worms
As he stands there in it with silver feet,
And those who died enter from barren rooms.

O you psalms in fiery midnight rains,
As the servants whipped soft eyes with nettles,
The childlike berries of the elder trees
Hang wide-eyed over an empty grave.

The yellowed moons softly revolve
Above the fevered sheets of the youth,
Before the silence of the winter comes.

A sublime fate contemplates down the Kidron,
Where the cedar, a soft creature,
Unfolds beneath the blue brows of the father,
Across the pasture a shepherd leads his flock at night.
Or there are screams in sleep,
When a bronze angel lines the people up in the grove,
The flesh of the saint melts on the searing grill.

Crimson grapes creep around cottages of burnt clay,
Sheaves sounding of yellowed grain,
The humming of bees, the flight of the crane.
With evening the resurrected find each other on stone paths.

Lepers see themselves in the black water;
Or they open their shit-spattered robes
Crying in the balsam wind that blows from pink hills.

Lithe country girls grope along the lanes of the night,
As though they would find their devoted herdsmen.
Saturdays gentle singing is heard in the cottages.

Let this song be in memory of the boy too,
His madness and white brows and his demise,
The one decayed who opens his eyes bluishly.
O how sad is this meeting again.

The degrees of madness in black rooms,
The shadows of the old ones under open doors,
There Helian's soul reveals itself in the pink mirror
And snow and leprosy drop from his forehead.

The stars are extinguished on the walls
And the white shapes of the light.

Skeletons emerge from their graves in the carpet,
That silence of falling crosses on the hill
The incense's sweetness in the purple night wind.

O you shattered eyes in black mouths,
As this descendent in a mellow blackout
Contemplates the darker end alone,
The still God lowers his blue lids above him.

Notes

PAGE 3 | 'The Ravens'

Line 1, *valley* (*Winkel*), the original (literally, angle) is a geographic—but still an abstract, shape-shifting—term here and synonymous with *Mulde* (small valley, hollow, gorge) and *Becken* (basin), and can also mean any opening or parting in a landscape, including an angled section of cultivated land braced by forest, as well as any hidden, remote place or void.

PAGE 4 | 'The Young Maid'

Dedication, *Ludwig von Ficker* (1880–1967), Austrian writer and publisher of the literary journal *Der Brenner*. Mentored Trakl as well as published and promoted his work and legacy.

PAGE 12 | 'Music in the Mirabell'

Second version, originally titled 'Colourful Autumn' ('Farbiger Herbst').

Title, *Mirabell*, a palace and public sculpture garden in Salzburg built in 1606 by the Prince-Bishop Wolf Dietrich von Raitenau for his mistress Salome Alt.

PAGE 14 | 'Winter Twilight'

Dedication, *Max von Esterle* (1870–1947), Austrian painter and caricaturist; member of *Der Brenner* circle. Befriended Trakl in 1911 and allowed him to use his studio to paint his self-portrait in 1913.

PAGE 16 | 'Boon of Women'

Line 11, *a black man (Moor)*, cf. *blackamoor*, an Expressionist usage, describing an Austrian peasant with tanned or sunburnt skin.

PAGE 22 | 'Evening Muse'

Line 15, *Endymion*, in classical mythology, the handsome youth who must sleep through his immortality and assignations with the moon goddess.

PAGE 23 | 'Dream of Evil'

First of three versions.

PAGE 28 | 'The Peasants'

Line 18, *stormy sea of wheat ears (tosenden Ährengebraus)*, the first word in the neologism *Ährengebraus* means wheat ears, tassels of grain, corn and the like; *Gebraus* means *roar*, specifically that of a storm on water, and is often a synonym for the same in German poetry.

PAGE 30 | 'All Souls'

Dedication, *Karl Hauer* (1875–1919), Austrian essayist, polemicist and bohemian.

Line 1, *Little husbands, wives (Die Männlein, Weiblein)*, the idiom suggests the Austrian custom of children's processions into the cemeteries on 2 November, All Souls' Day, in order to tend family graves.

PAGE 34 | 'Valley in the Forest'

Title, see note to 'The Ravens'.

Dedication, *Karl Minnich* (1886–1964), a classmate of Trakl and one of his intimates and drinking companions in Salzburg.

PAGE 36 | 'In an Old Guest Book'

Title, *Guest Book (Stammbuch)*, an allusion to the old custom of collecting the autographs, wishes, sentimental verses and drawings by friends, relatives and family members.

PAGE 37 | 'Metamorphosis'

Second of two versions.

Line 6, *One emerging* (*Erscheinender*), in the sense of an imago.

PAGE 38 | 'Concertino'

Line 13, *Daedalus*, the craftsman of mythology, who designed the Labyrinth and the wings for himself and his son Icarus.

PAGE 41 | 'The Walk'

Line 6, *A buoyant number stands up on a stone*, a milestone.

Line 13, *Helios*, the Greek god who personifies the sun.

Line 16, *gold-hammers* (*Goldammern*), songbirds that nest in thickets and whose call inspired the opening notes of Beethoven's Fifth Symphony.

Line 35, *Rachel*, wife of Jacob in the Book of Genesis, whose long inability to conceive a child is evoked in the poem.

PAGE 44 | 'De Profundis'

Title, *De Profundis*, the penitential opening line of the Latin text of Psalm 130, meaning 'from the depths'.

PAGE 46 | 'Trumpets'

Line 3, *Banners of scarlet* (*Fahnen von Scharlach*), an allusion to the red flags indicating that a neighbourhood was quarantined for scarlet fever (*Scharlach* means scarlet fever in German).

PAGE 48 | 'Bright Spring'

Second of two versions.

PAGE 53 | 'The Rats'

Line 12, *howl* (*greinen*), can also be translated to describe the shape of the mouth when making such a sound—indeed, it is a close cognate of grin and grimace; so the howl here can be one of protest, grief, laughter and the like.

First of two versions.

Second of two versions.

Dedication, *Karl Kraus* (1874–1936), Austrian writer, polemicist and cultural journalist.

Line 37, *Golgotha*, Aramaic name of Calvary whose meaning is derived from the skull-pan shape of the hill.

'To My Sister'

Title, *Sister*, i.e. Margarete Jeanne Trakl (1891–1917).

'Nearness of Death'

Second of two versions.

'Amen'

Line 8, *Azrael*, the archangel of death.

Second version, originally titled 'Autumn'.

Line 7, *sundial* (*Stunden Weiser*), can be also rendered as *clock* and *hour hands,* as well as a sundial's gnomon. The meaning used here is based on the belief that sundials were infallible vis-à-vis clockwork and thus came with admonition, either implicit or inscribed, that God was so infallible in pointing out the hour of one's death.

Dedication, *Karl Röck*, the pseudonym of Guido Höld (1883–1954), an Austrian writer.

Second of three versions.

Title and line 24, the anagram of *Misery* (*Elend*) in the title and *ennobled's* (*Edlen*) in the last line cannot be rendered.

Dedication, *Erhard Buschbeck* (1889–1960), Austrian writer and dramatist and a childhood friend of Trakl.

Line 20, *leprosy*, a dysromantic trope for decay and decline. Although leprosy had died out in most of Europe in the late nineteenth and early twentieth centuries, 'leprosy villages' existed in remote districts, where observers simply noted a high incidence of so-called hereditary skin diseases, including syphilis (categorized with leprosy in the primary nineteenth-century German medical text). Leprosy was much discussed during Trakl's time, especially given the new cases of the so-called Norwegian leprosy as well as in missionary lands, which suggested that the dread biblical scourge had not been eradicated in Europe and would return. For this reason, Trakl is merely *au courant* in this poem rather than arcane.

Line 5, *Elai*, from the Aramaic for 'my God,' a supplication found in Psalm 22:5 and quoted by the crucified Christ in Matthew 27:46 and Mark 15:34 ('My God, my God, why have you forsaken me?').

Title, *Helian*, Latin for the Greek name Helios, a sun god, and one of Trakl's personae.

Line 61, *Kidron*, a stream that flows through the valley of the same name along the eastern wall of Jerusalem that separates it from the Mount of Olives.